THE PEOPLE OF THE
PHILIPPINES

Dolly Brittan

The Rosen Publishing Group's
PowerKids Press™
New York

Published in 1997 by The Rosen Publishing Group, Inc.
29 East 21st Street, New York, NY 10010

First Edition

Book Design: Danielle Primiceri

Photo Credits: Cover (background) © Cliff Hollenbeck/International Stock, (front) © AP/Wide World Photos; pp. 4, 7, 8, 20 © Cliff Hollenbeck/International Stock; pp. 11, 12 (inset), 16, 19 (all) © Joe Viesti/Viesti Associates, Inc.; pp. 12 (background), 15 © Mark Downey/Viesti Associates, Inc.

Brittan, Dolly.
    The people of the Philippines / Dolly Brittan.
        p. cm. (Celebrating the peoples and civilizations of Southeast Asia)
    Summary: Introduces the culture, religion, and beliefs of the people of the Philippines, as well as the landscape of their country.
    ISBN 0-8239-5127-8
    1. Philippines—Juvenile literature. [1. Philippines.] I. Title. II. Series.
    DS655.B75 1997
    959.9—dc21
                                               96-8377
                                             CIP
                                             AC

Contents

The Philippines

The **Philippines** (FIL-ih-peenz) is a country in the Pacific Ocean near Southeast Asia. Its official name is the Republic of the Philippines. The people of the Philippines are **Filipinos** (fil-ih-PEEN-ohz).

Over 7,000 islands make up the Philippines. People live on 2,000 of the islands. The Philippines is divided into three main areas: Luzon, the Visayas, and Mindanao. The capital of the Philippines, Manila, is on Luzon, which is also the biggest island.

◄ *Only half of the islands that make up the Philippines have names. This is the island of Legaspi.*

A Long History

Most Filipinos are **descendents** (dee-SEN-dents) of people from Malaysia who traveled to the Philippines hundreds of years ago. Explorer Ferdinand Magellan led the first group of Europeans to the Philippines in 1521. Spanish explorer López de Villalobos followed in 1542. He named the islands the Philippines after Philip II, the prince of Spain.

The Philippines were ruled by Spain until 1898, when the islands were turned over to the United States. The United States governed until 1946, when it granted the Philippines its **independence** (in-dee-PEN-dents).

Many Filipinos live on the coast of their islands. ▶

Made by Volcanoes

There are 37 **volcanoes** (vol-KAY-nohz) in the Philippines. Twelve of them are **active** (AK-tiv). Most of the islands were made by volcanoes. The highest volcano peak is Mount Apo, which is 9,690 feet high. Most of the larger islands have mountain ranges that are made up of volcanoes.

The Philippines are hot and humid all year. In the lowlands, it is about 80°F. In the mountains, or highlands, it is cooler. The temperature there is about 65°F.

Mayon Volcano, which is on the island of Legaspi, is the most active volcano in the Philippines. It has erupted 47 times since 1616.

Farming and Fishing

The warm, wet **climate** (KLY-met) and the rich soil in the Philippines are great for growing crops. The main crops are rice, corn, coconut, sugarcane, sweet potatoes, and bananas. Some farmers raise animals, such as pigs, chickens, goats, ducks, and water buffalo.

There are thousands of kinds of fish in the ocean surrounding the Philippines. Filipino fishermen catch many different kinds of fish, such as tuna, swordfish, shrimp, and anchovies. By tradition, some Filipino fishermen cover their faces with cloths so they do not scare the fish.

Rice is one of the main crops of the Philippines, ▶
as in many other countries in Southeast Asia.

Culture and Religion

The **culture** (KUL-cher) of the Philippines is a blend of Spanish, American, Chinese, and **native** (NAY-tiv) customs. **Traditional** (truh-DISH-un-ul) Filipino theater, **literature** (LIT-er-uh-cher), and *kundiman*, or love songs, as well as American music and television shows, are enjoyed throughout the Philippines.

Over 90 percent of Filipinos are Christian. Much of the remaining 10 percent of Filipinos follow other religions, such as Islam or Buddhism.

◀ *Making bamboo furniture and weaving cloth with brightly colored threads are two traditional crafts that some Filipinos still practice.*

The Language

There are over 70 languages spoken in the Philippines. But the official language is Pilipino. A traditional greeting in Pilipino is "**Mabuhay** (muh-BOO-hay)!" This can mean "welcome," "farewell," or "good luck." Many Filipinos also speak English, and a few speak Spanish.

Filipinos often speak with their eyes, lips, and hands as well as with their voices. Raised eyebrows and a smile mean "hello" or "yes" in answer to a question.

Many Filipinos like to communicate with their expressions. ▶

Food

Filipino food is a blend of Chinese, Malay, and Spanish cooking. Most meals are served with rice. Some dishes are made with meats and vegetables cooked with vinegar and garlic. Other dishes include meat stews and many kinds of soups, such as rice, noodle, beef, chicken, and sour vegetable soup. Barbecued sticks of meat or seafood are sometimes served as evening snacks. *Halo-halo* is a favorite dessert made from sweets, fruit, and milk mixed with crushed ice.

Filipinos enjoy the flavors of Chinese, Malay, and Spanish foods in their meals.

Celebrations

There are celebrations and festivals held nearly every week in different parts of the Philippines. One important festival is **Pahiyas** (puh-HEE-yus). This celebrates the feast day of the **patron saint** (PAY-trun SAYNT) of farmers. During Pahiyas, people give thanks for a good **harvest** (HAR-vest).

Independence Day is celebrated on June 12th with parades and flags. And New Year's Day is filled with food, fireworks, music, and dancing.

The biggest festival in the Philippines is Ati-Atihan. Ati-Atihan is held during the third week of January on the island of Panay. It is a celebration of a traditional festival and the Christian saint, Santo Niño.

Music and Dance

Most celebrations are filled with music, song, and dance. Many Filipinos enjoy traditional music as well as Western music. Traditional Filipino musical instruments include the bamboo guitar, the nose flute, and *kulintang*, or gongs. Filipino dances are often a mix of Malay and Spanish dances. Two popular dances are the *singkil* and *jota*. Singing and dancing contests are often held during festivals.

Dancers wear colorful costumes that are a blend of styles of clothing from different cultures.

The Philippines Today

The people of the Philippines have a long history of tradition and change. Over the last 500 years, they have had to adjust to outside **influences** (IN-floo-ent-sez) in their country. Along the way, they have lost many native traditions. But they have also created new ones. Today, the culture of the people of the Philippines is a blend of the many countries that have influenced it. As Filipinos travel and move to different countries around the world, they share their culture and new traditions.

Glossary

active (AK-tiv) Able to erupt.

climate (KLY-met) The weather.

culture (KUL-cher) The customs, tools, and religions of a group of people.

descendent (dee-SEN-dent) A person born of a certain group of people.

Filipino (fil-ih-PEEN-oh) A person who lives in the Philippines.

harvest (HAR-vest) A season's gathered crop.

independence (in-dee-PEN-dents) The act of freeing yourself from the control of someone else.

influence (IN-floo-ents) A person or country that has an effect on others.

literature (LIT-er-uh-cher) The writings of a period of time or of a country.

mabuhay (muh-BOO-hay) A greeting in the Pilipino language.

native (NAY-tiv) From, grown, or produced in a certain area.

Pahiyas (puh-HEE-yus) A Filipino holiday.

patron saint (PAY-trun SAYNT) A saint that guards or protects.

Philippines (FIL-ih-peenz) A country made up of islands in the South China Sea, near Southeast Asia.

traditional (truh-DISH-un-ul) A way of doing something that is passed down from parent to child.

volcano (vol-KAY-noh) A cone-shaped hill or mountain around an opening in the earth's crust through which steam, ashes, and lava are sometimes forced out.

23

Index